Meditative Coloring Book 1:

ANGELS

Aliyah Schick

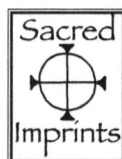

Sacred
Imprints

Other Books by Aliyah Schick

- *Mary Magdalene's Words: Two Women's Spiritual Journey, Both Truth and Fiction, Both Ancient and Now.*
- *Meditative Coloring Book 2: Crosses*
- *Meditative Coloring Book 3: Ancient Symbols*
- *Meditative Coloring Book 4: Hearts*
- *Meditative Coloring Book 5: Labyrinths*
- *Finally, a Book of Poetry by Aliyah Schick*

ISBN: 978-0-9844125-2-5

www.MeditativeColoring.com

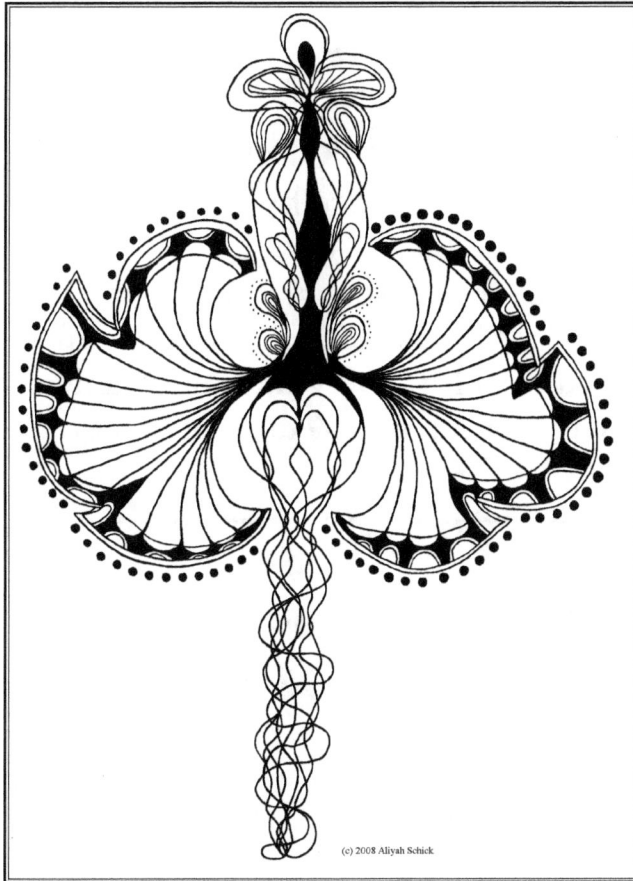
(c) 2008 Aliyah Schick

Table of Contents

What Are Angelic Imprints?

Each of these original pen-and-ink drawings is a unique work of art created through spiritual guidance by artist/healer Aliyah Schick.

Aliyah begins with a centering meditation. With a pen in each hand, she allows the lines to go where they will, dancing their designs, the two sides mirroring each other. Every movement is guided by spirit. Every drawing is different and each one is a wonderful surprise. Once the form is complete, details are added with her dominant hand.

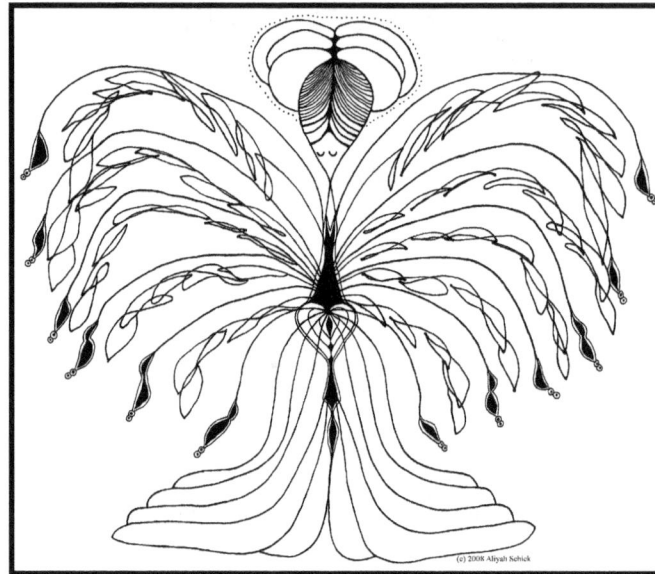

A simple, brain-balancing drawing exercise first opened the way. Free flowing line and form quickly evolved into more than pleasing harmony. Before she knew it, and much to her surprise, Aliyah found herself drawing angel energy.

Angelic Imprints bring remarkable responses.

- They can move you deeply,
- They may open your intuitive vision,
- Help you recognize your spiritual potential,
- And put you in touch with your higher self.

Most importantly, they can remind you of who you really are. Neale Donald Walsch and others say this remembrance is a very important goal for your life on earth.

Angels

Nearly every culture and religion on earth has included angels in stories and beliefs. From as far back as 3,000 B.C.E. angels have been depicted in art and writings as winged messengers between God and humans, helping us in our lives.

One poll in the U.S. showed that 68% of Americans believe that angels are active in the world. Another survey found that 55% of Americans believe a guardian angel has protected them during their life.

The number of people learning about and connecting with angels has greatly increased in the past 20 years. Over 5 million angel-related books have been sold, plus innumerable workshops and programs offered, and gatherings created. Angel art and products fill more than 100 specialty stores and catalogs. We are more interested in and receptive to these heavenly beings than ever before.

Here are just a few examples:

• August 22nd is national "Be an Angel Day."

• Doreen Virtue brings many thousands of people each year to angel awareness through her workshops, radio programs, her many books including *Angels 101: An Introduction to Connecting, Working, and Healing with the Angels,* and the network of thousands of Angel Therapy Practitioners she has trained.

• In the 1990 classic *Messengers of Light* author Terry Lynn Taylor describes angels as "ever-helpful messengers of divine providence…heaven-sent agents who are always available to help you create heaven on earth." Her book explains what angels are, who they are, and how to attract and interact with them.

• *Ask Your Angels,* by Daniel, Wiley, and Ramer, teaches us how to talk with our angels using a simple 5-step method called the GRACE process.

• Jean Slatter's *Hiring the Heavens: A Practical Guide to Developing Working Relationships with the Spirits of Creation* has helped many people learn to ask angels to help in all sorts of ways in their lives.

Suggestions for How to Use This Book

Use this *Sacred Imprints Meditative Coloring Book* for spiritual connection, prayer, relaxation, healing, centering, and for coming into your deep, true self. You may simply wish to experience the images in quiet contemplation. Or, you may focus on a prayer or affirmation as you work with colors. You may ask for understanding regarding an issue you are dealing with. You may ask for a clearer sense of some aspect of yourself and how it serves you. You may wish to learn about your path or purpose in this lifetime.

Open your heart and your mind as you use this *Sacred Imprints Meditative Coloring Book*. Pay attention to impressions and ideas, feelings, intuition, and messages. They may very well be exactly what you need to hear.

Tools
Choose your favorite coloring tools, or you might like to gather a variety of pens, crayons, colored pencils, chalk, oil pastels, markers, glitter pens, paints, etc. You may want to place a blank sheet of paper behind the page so ink or paint does not go through.

Music
Consider playing soft instrumental or contemplative background music.

Nature
Sometimes a favorite spot outdoors provides just the right environment for creative expression. Beach, woods, backyard, porch, treehouse, mountain top, stream, pond, park, etc.

Silence
You may prefer quiet, so that all your attention focuses on what you are doing. Emptiness can give rise to profound experience.

Meditation
You may like to meditate first, and then begin working with the colors. Try any of the many ways of meditation, or simply be with your breath for a few minutes, following it in and out. Or, you may wish to try the meditation offering on the next page. Read it silently or out loud, slowly, pausing to draw in each breath.

Meditation

Take in a breath... and on the exhale release the day's happenings, settling into this peaceful time of creative, spiritual connection.

Take in a breath... and on the exhale let go of worries and troubles and burdens. You can pick them up again later if you need to.

Take in a breath... and on the exhale come into the center of your Self. From there drop a line down through your body, through the chair and the floor and into the earth. Through soil and sand and stone, through coal and underground stream, and minerals and precious metals. Down through all the colors and textures and densities of the earth, down into the hot magma at this planet's core. Down to the very center of the earth, to the Heart of the Mother. Tie your line there. Anchor yourself there.

Take in a breath... and on the exhale extend your line up from your center, through your body and out the crown of your head, up through the roof and into the sky. Past clouds and wind and thinning gases, out through the atmosphere and into space. Past the sun and galaxy and stars and universe, out to the depths of the Source of All That Is. Feel your connection there. You are part of the great cosmos. You are one with all being.

Take in a breath... and on the exhale return to the drawing before you and ask that you be open to receiving guidance and understanding as you spend time with it. Know that there are no mistakes, only new choices and combinations and patterns that suggest new perception at an other-than-conscious level. Or that remind us of something that can now be released. Or that create an opening to new possibilities.

Take in a breath... and on the exhale release "shoulds" and rules and expectations. Let go and open to new possibilities.

Now, begin by picking up whatever color catches your attention.

About the Artist

Aliyah Schick has been an artist all of her life. After Peace Corps in the Andes Mountains of South America, she studied art full time for four years, then created and sold pottery and ceramic art pieces for many years. Later Aliyah worked in fiber and fabric, making soft sculptural wall pieces and art quilts, then fabric dolls designed to carry healing energy. Now she draws and paints, and she writes poems and prose.

At the heart of all this, Aliyah's real work is healing. She is a skilled and dynamic deep energetic healer and Transformation Coach. Her work in the multidimensional layers and patterns of the auric field is powerful and effective. The *Sacred Imprints* drawings, paintings, poetry, and writings, and the *Meditative Coloring Books* emerged as new expressions of Aliyah's healing abilities. Experiencing these drawings and working with them serves to remind us who we are, where we come from, and why we are here.

Aliyah lives and works in the beautiful Blue Ridge Mountains of North Carolina, where the energy of the earth is easily accessible, ancient, motherly, and obvious. A place where people speak with familiarity and reverence of the land and spirit, and where the sacred comes to sit with us on the porch to share the afternoon sun.

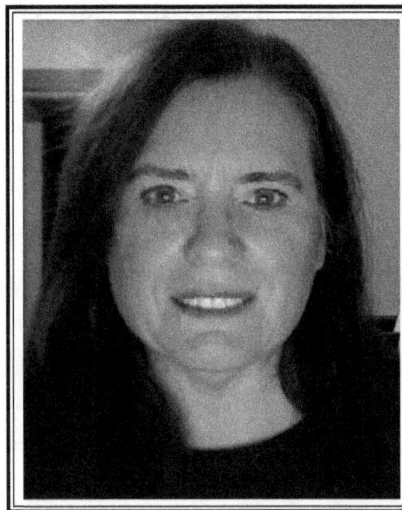

www.AliyahSchick.com

The Drawings

Opposite each drawing is a blank page labeled Meditative Impressions. Use these pages to catch and keep hold of your thoughts, wishes, intentions, affirmations, prayers, poems, memories, notes, drawings, or whatever comes to you as you explore coloring with this book. Make it yours.

Meditative Impressions

9

Meditative Impressions

(c)2008 Aliyah Schick

11

Meditative Impressions

13

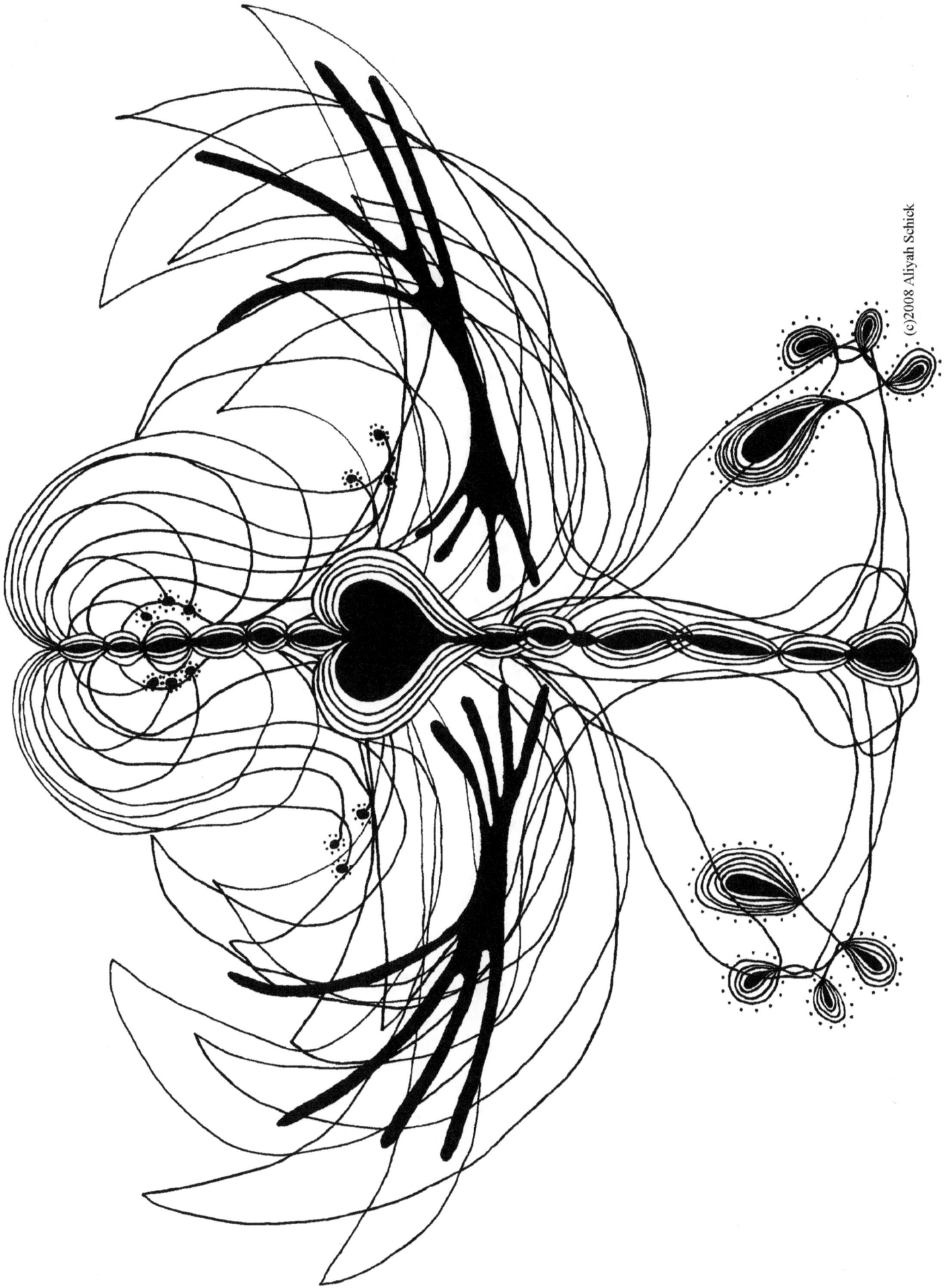

15

Meditative Impressions

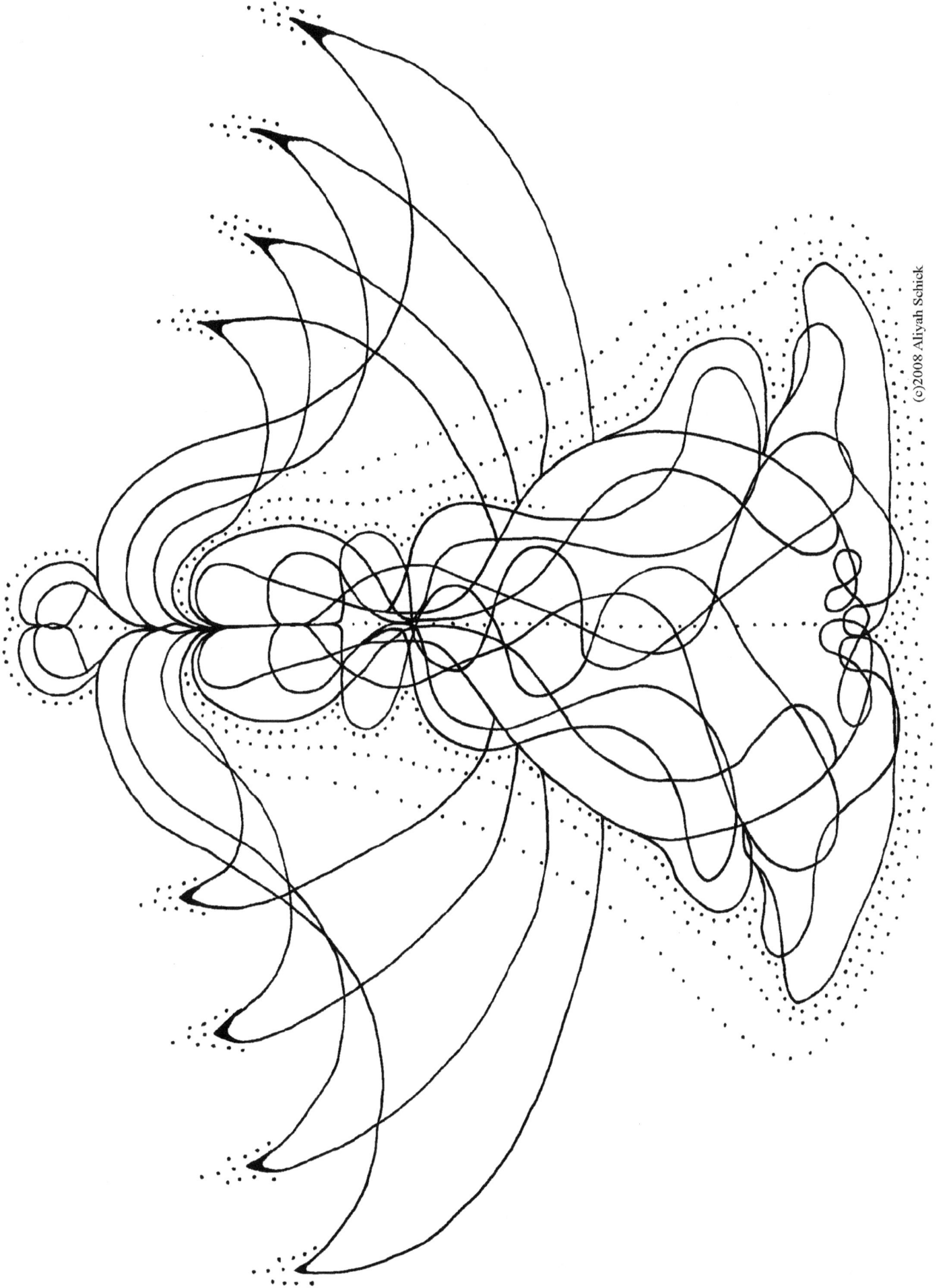

17

Meditative Impressions

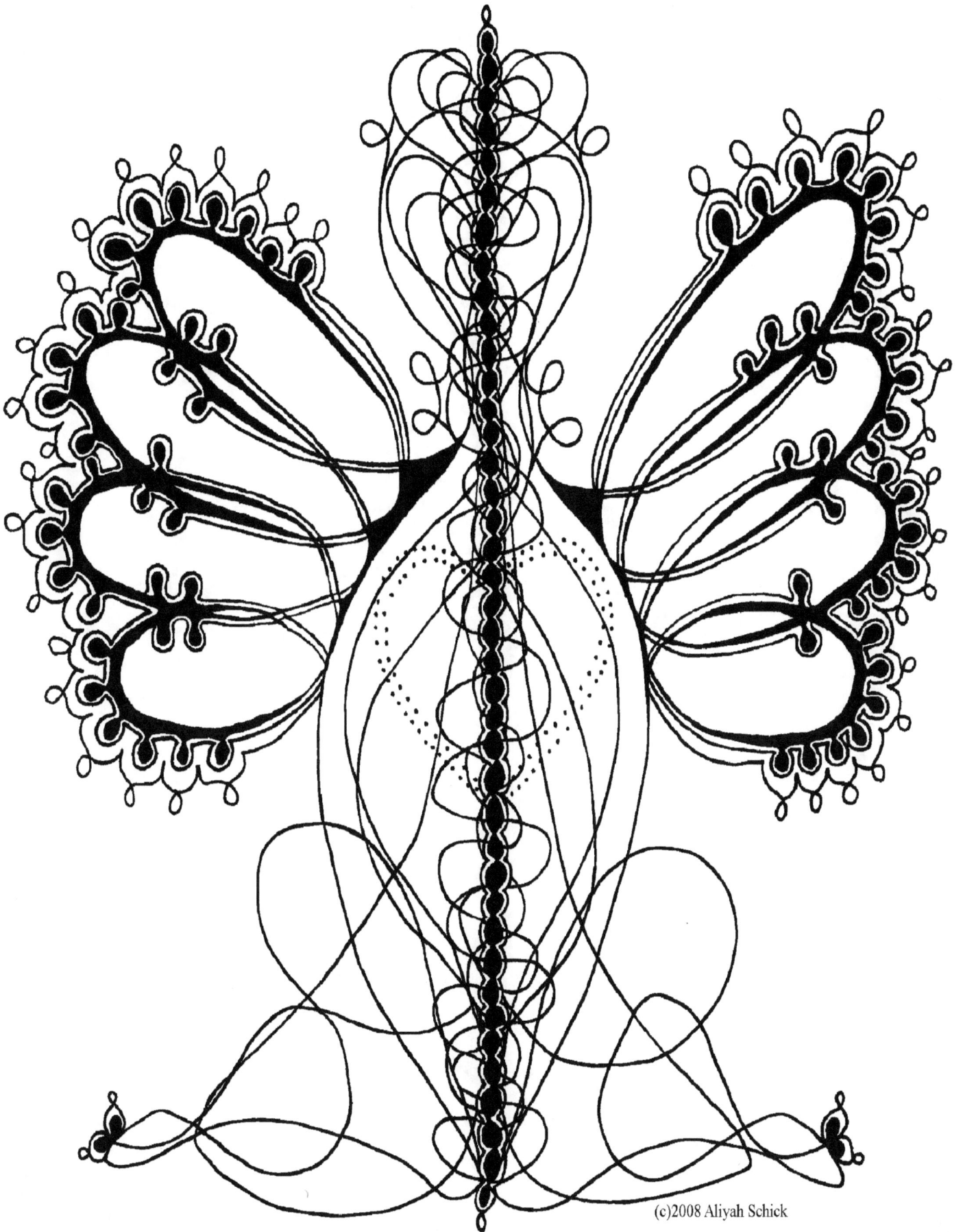

(c)2008 Aliyah Schick

Meditative Impressions

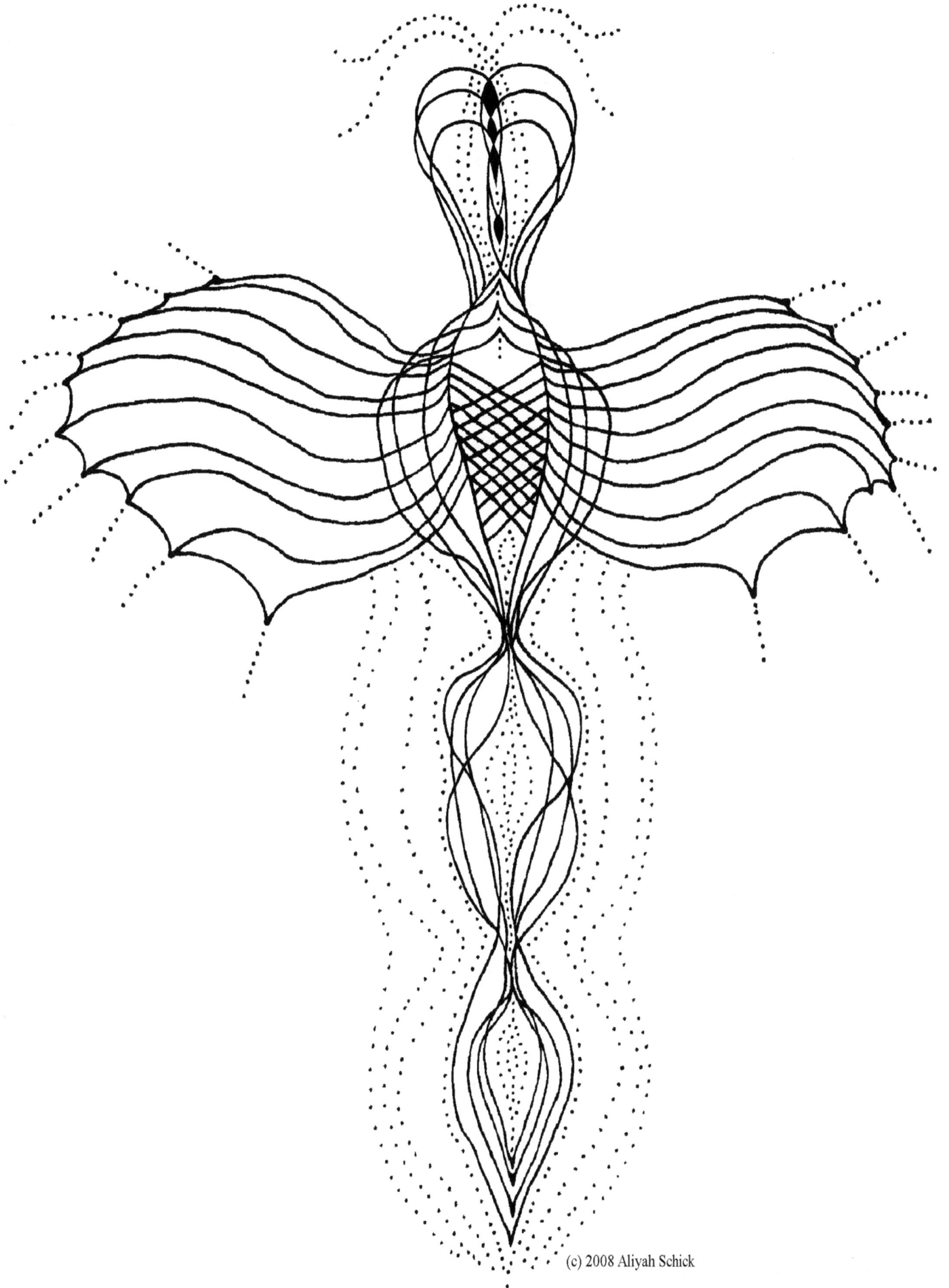

(c) 2008 Aliyah Schick

23

Meditative Impressions

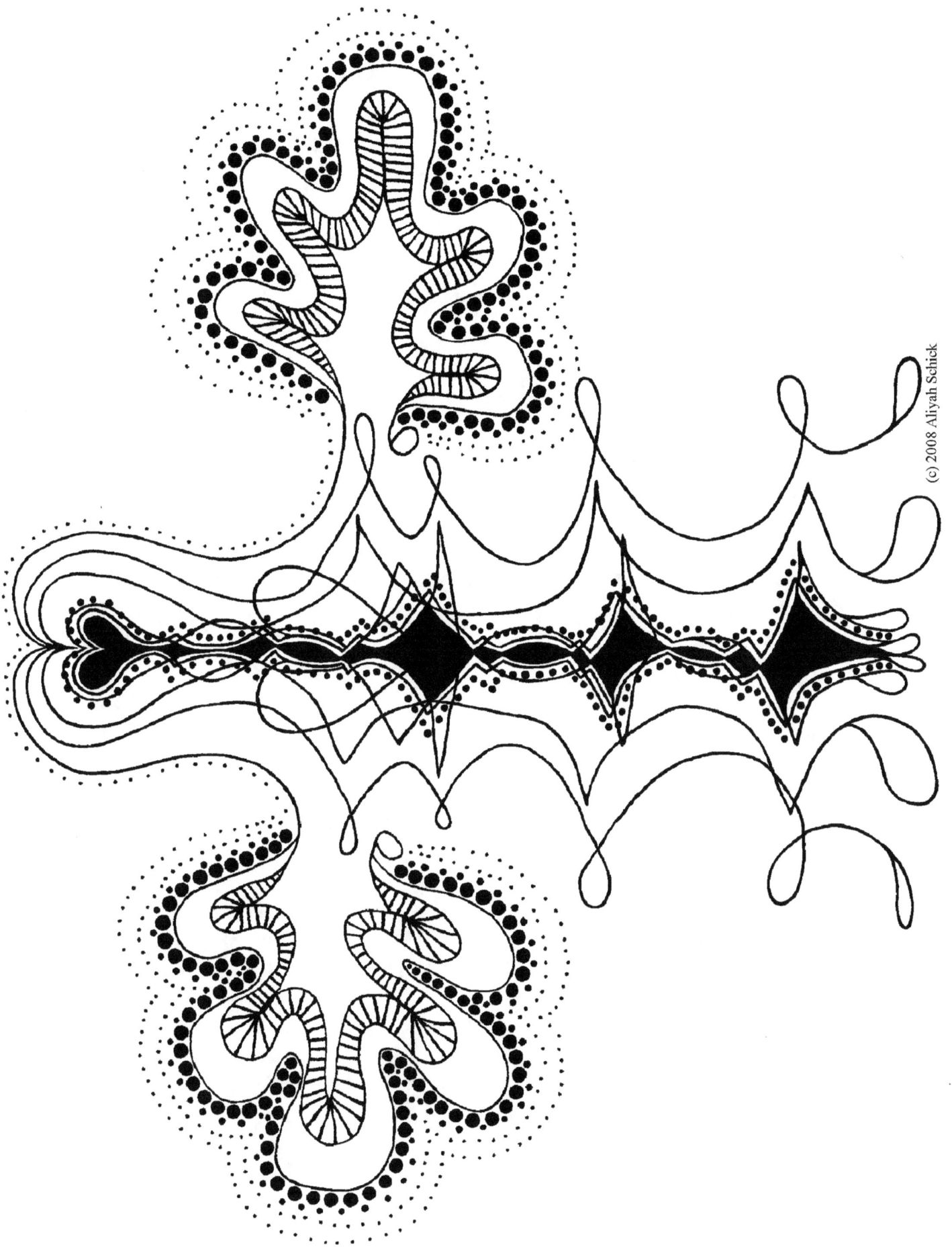

25

Meditative Impressions

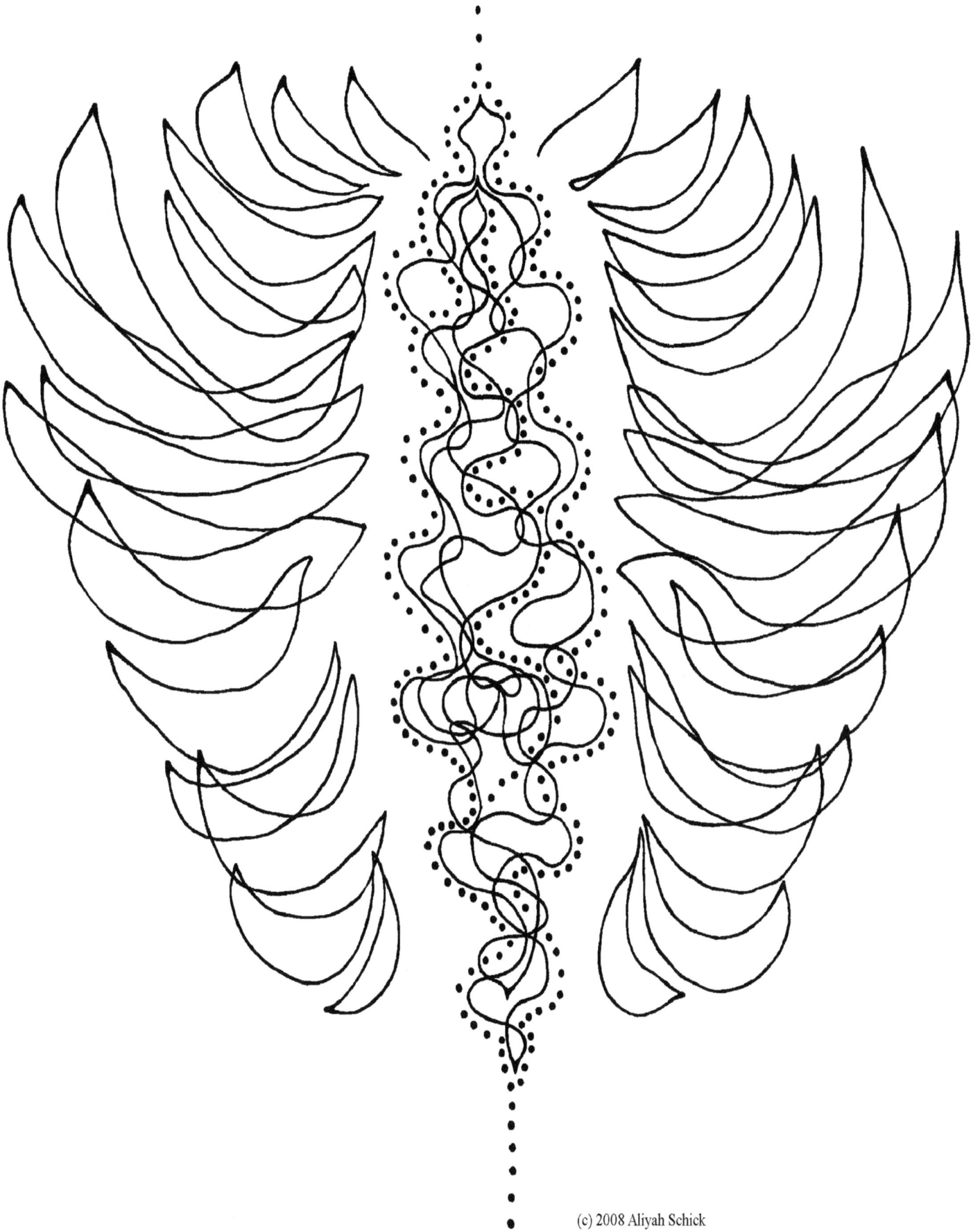

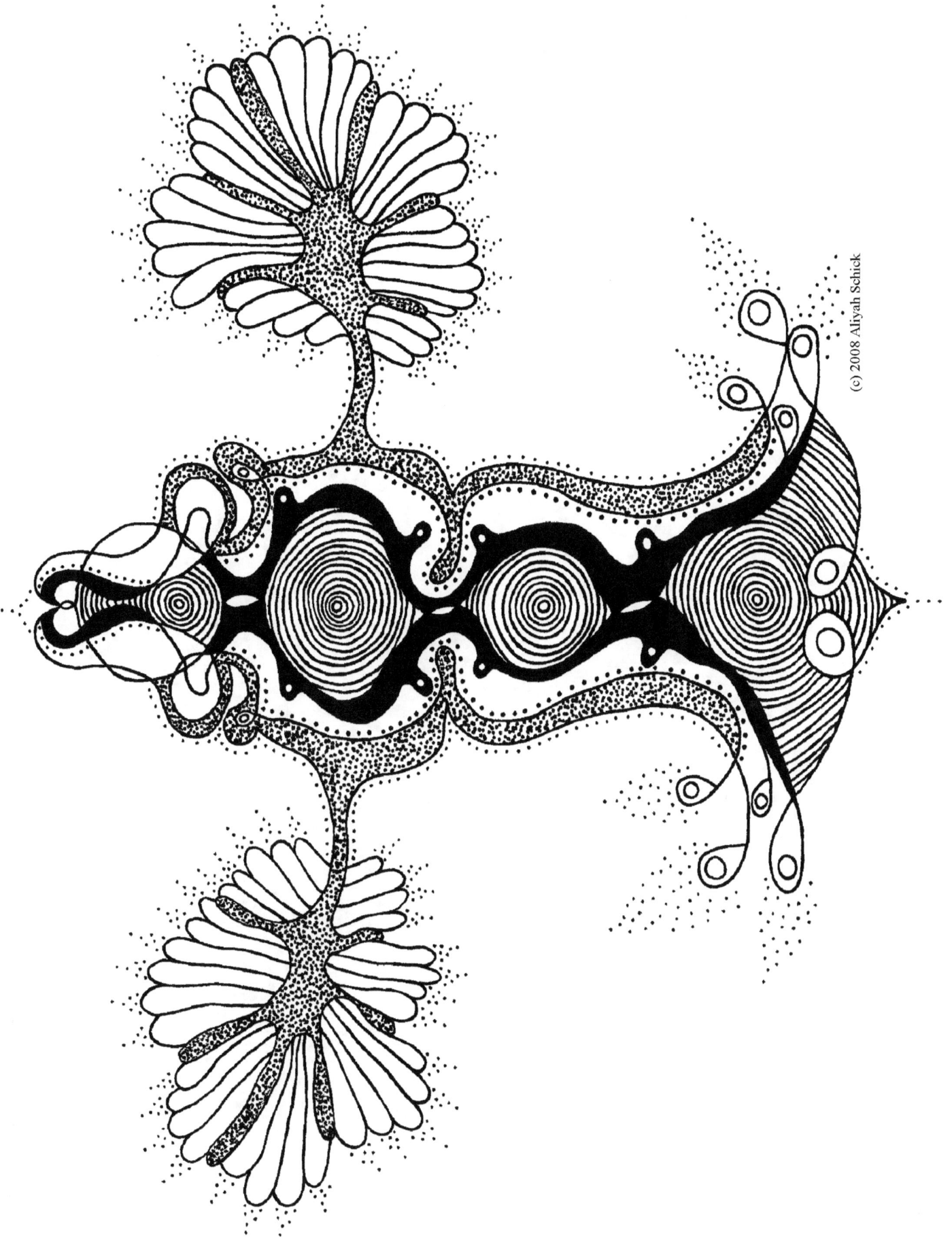

31

Meditative Impressions

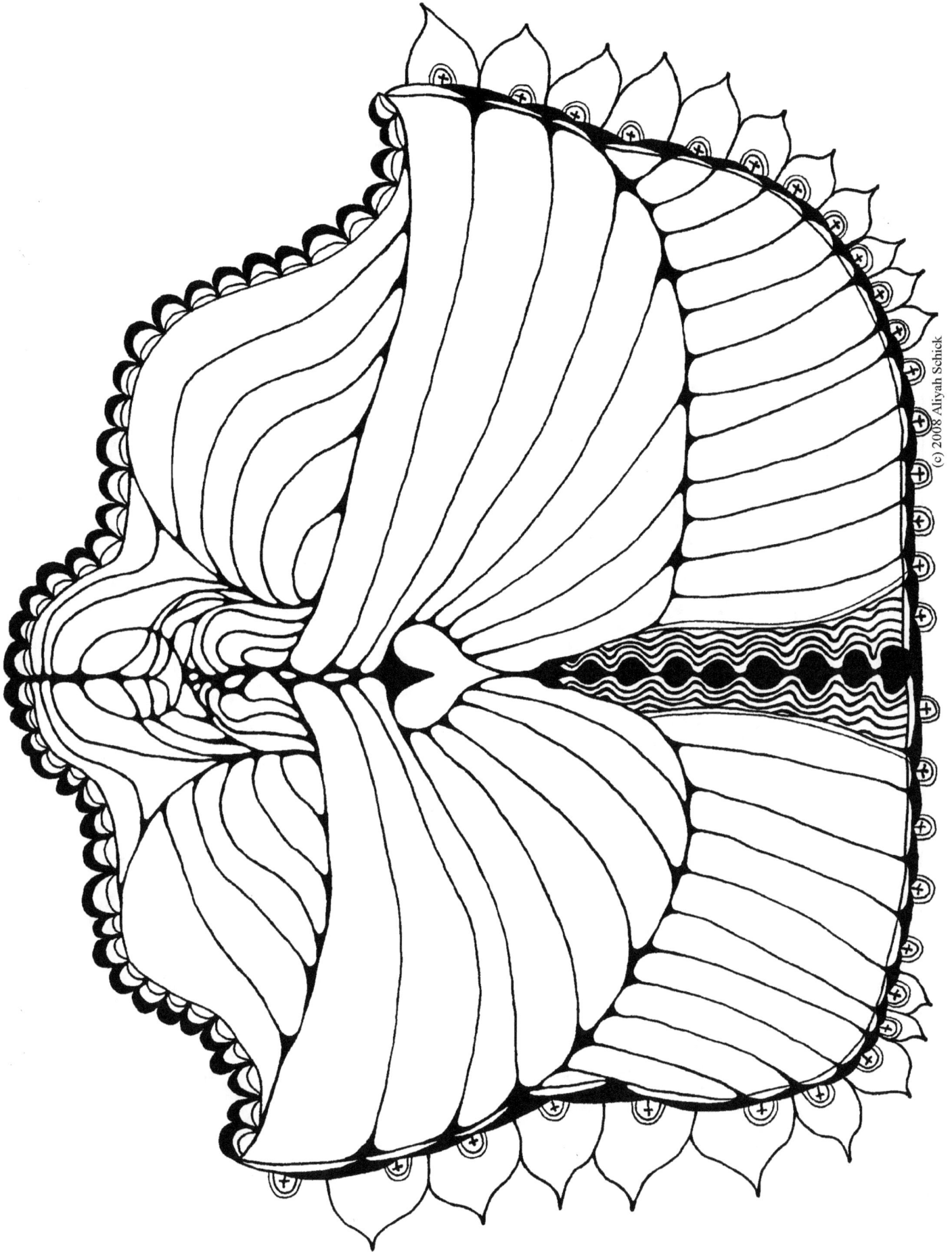

Meditative Impressions

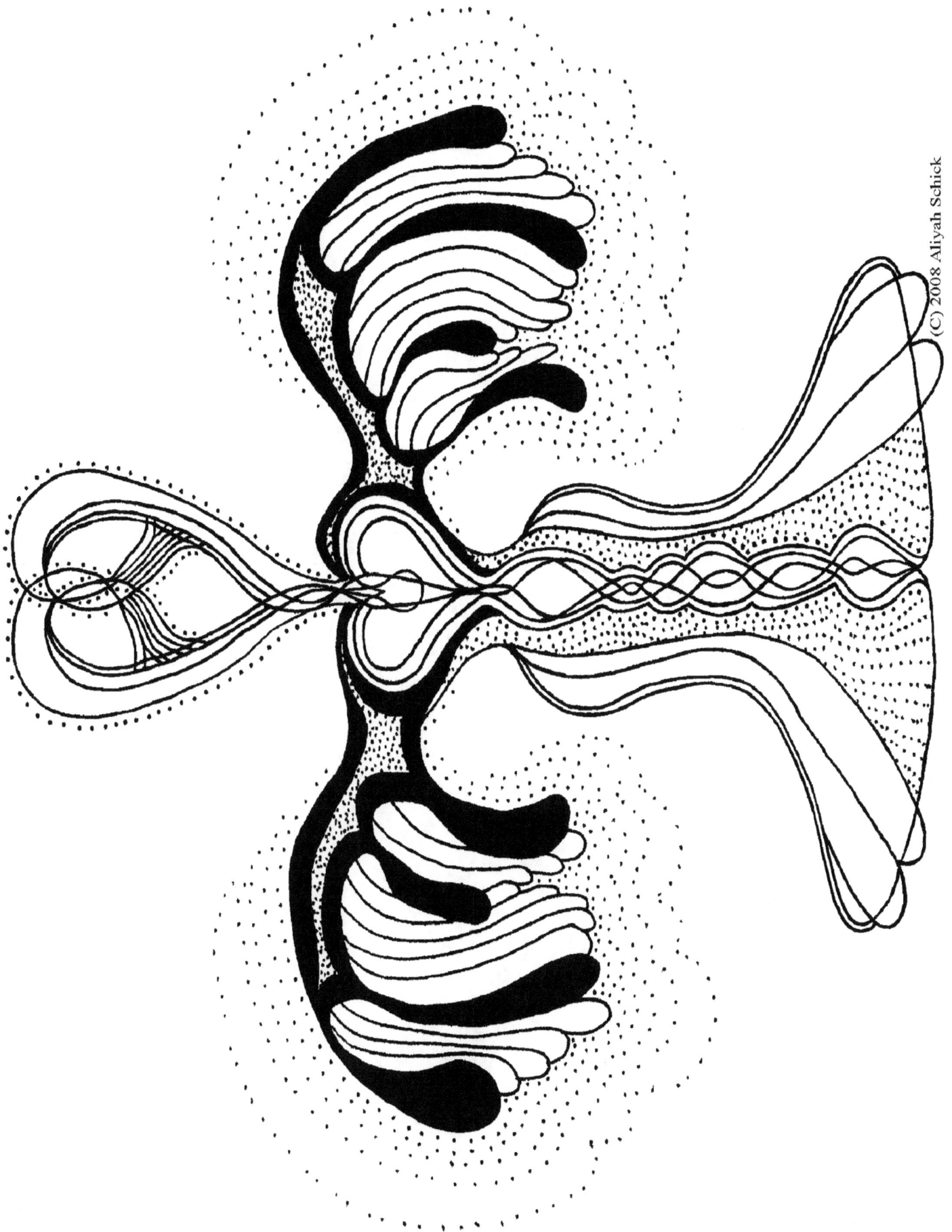

35

Meditative Impressions

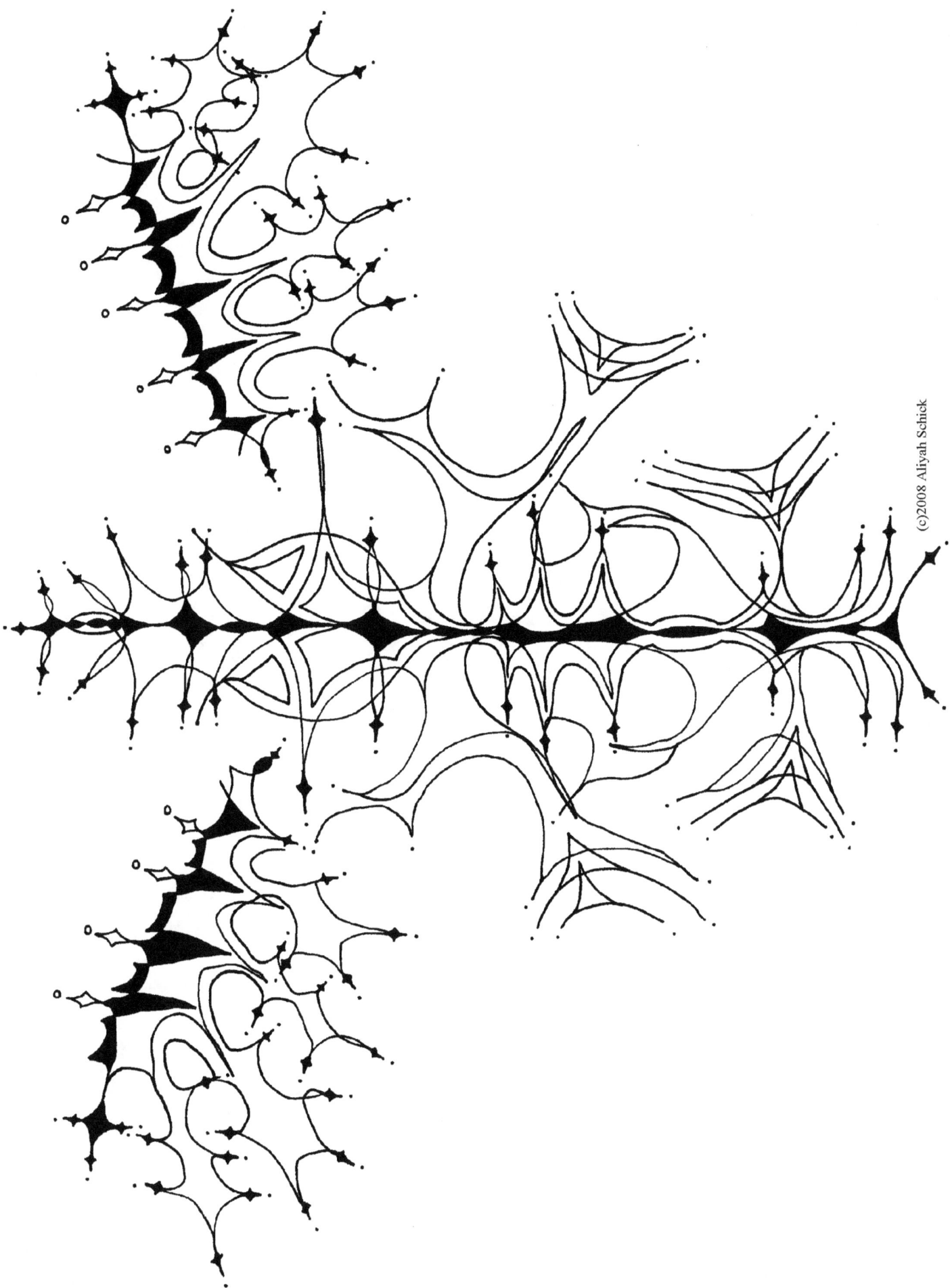

37

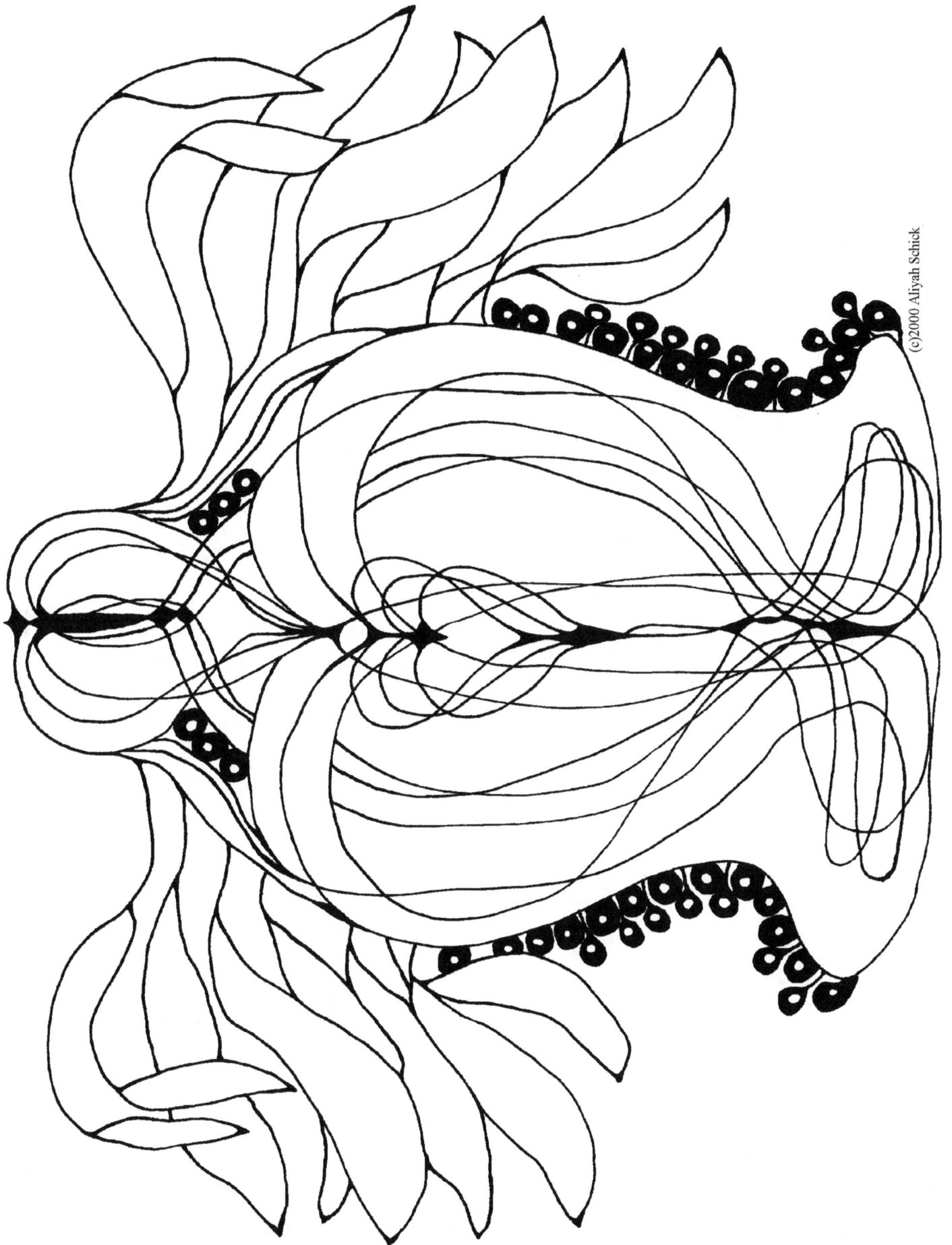

Meditative Impressions

41

Meditative Impressions

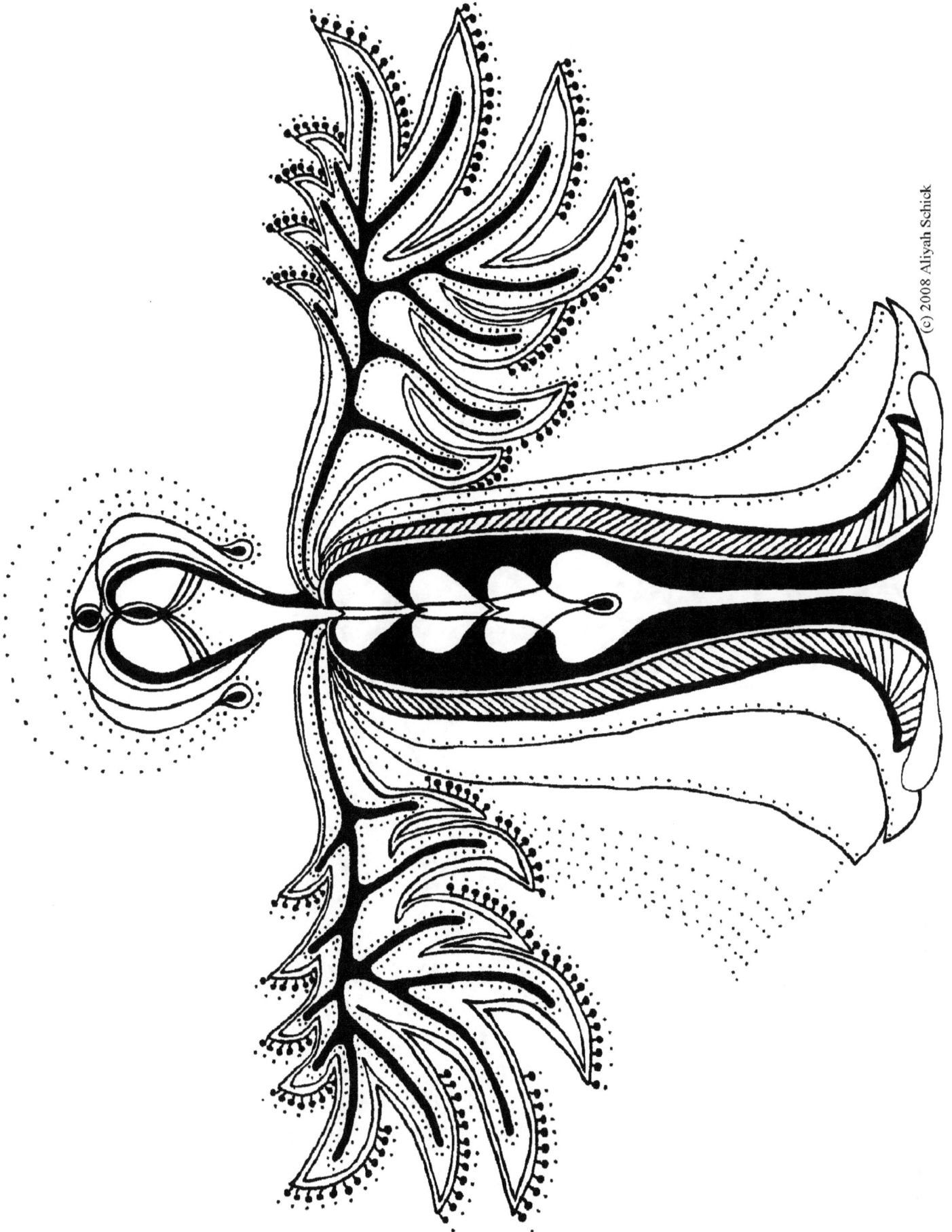

43

Meditative Impressions

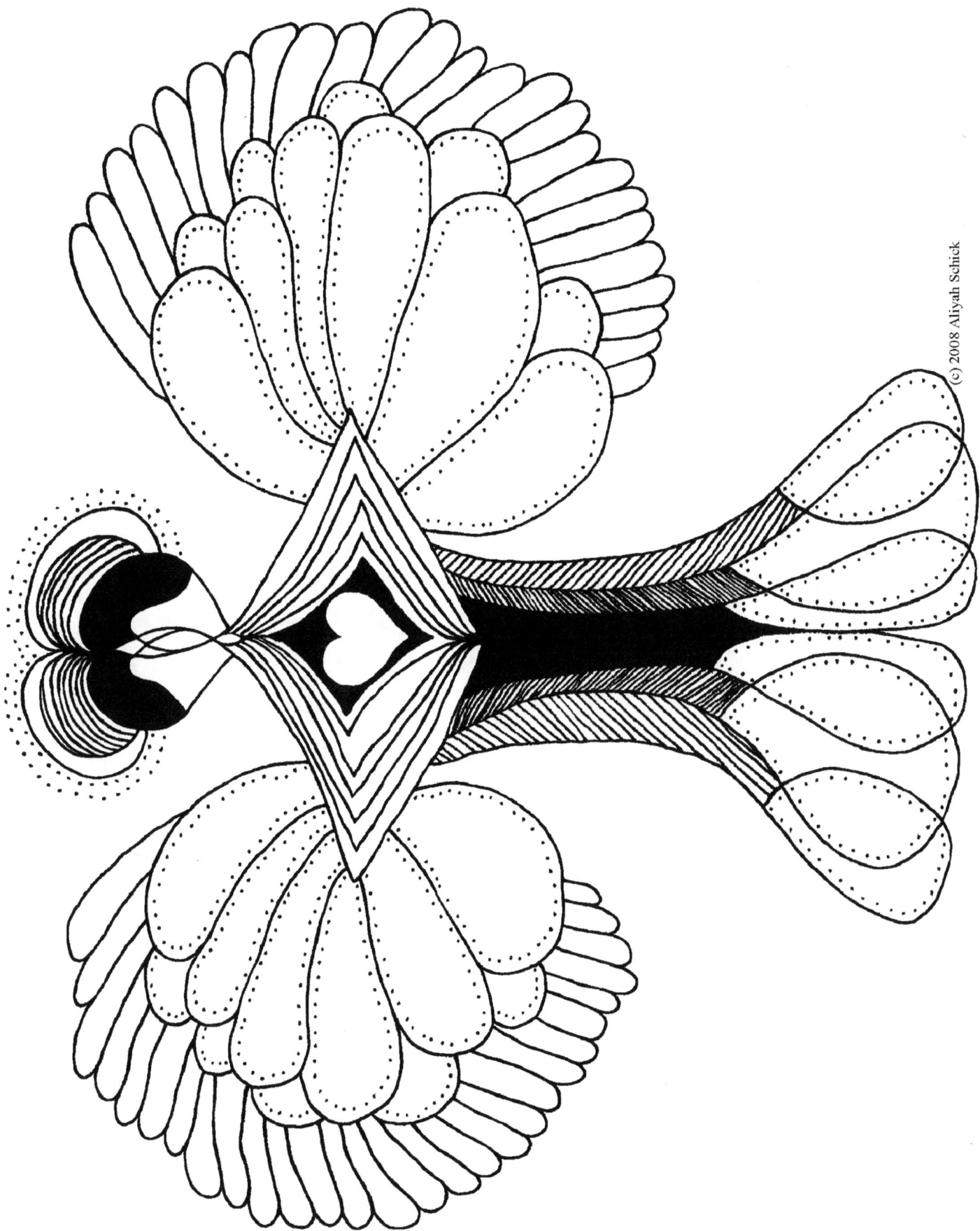

Meditative Impressions

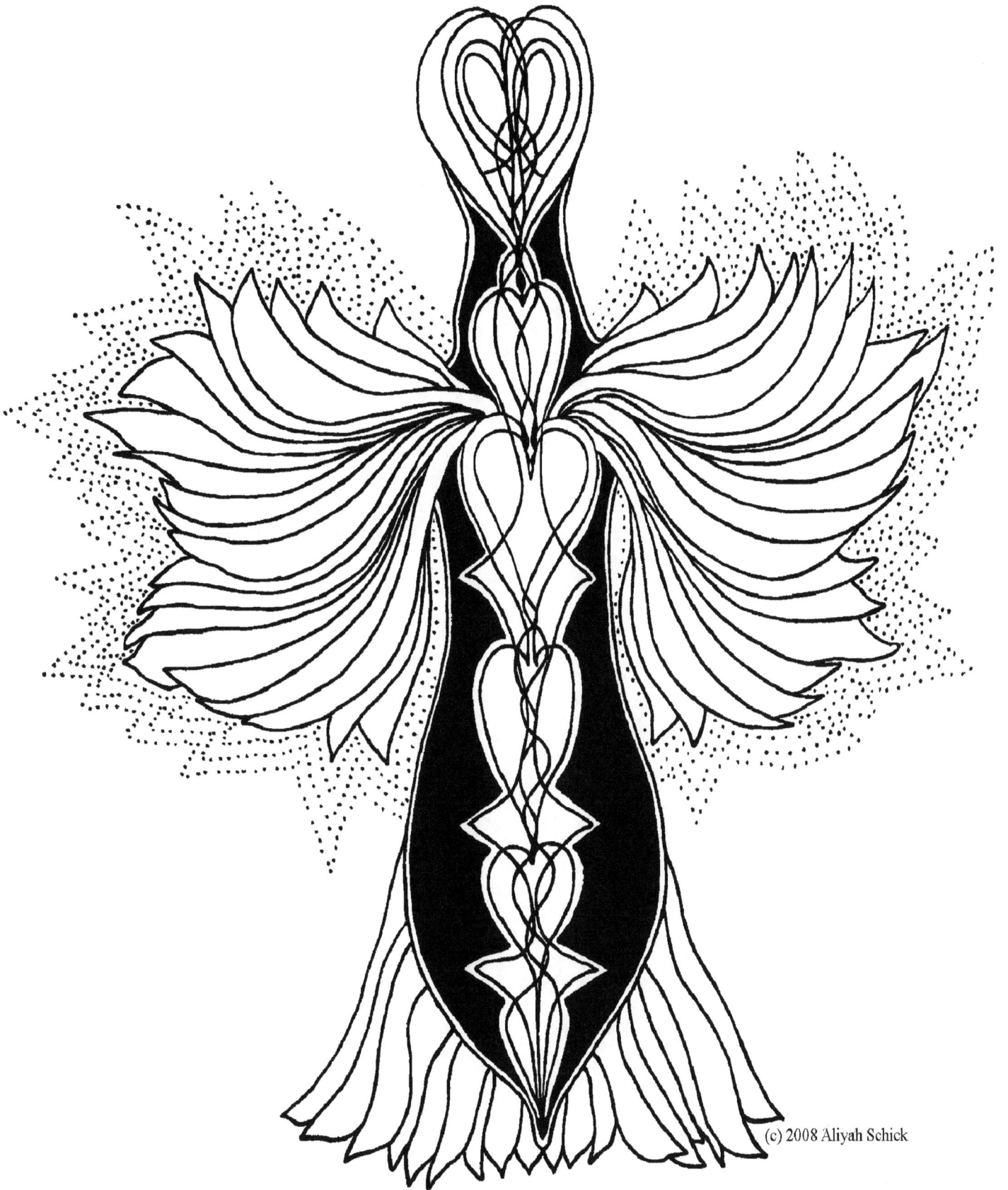

(c) 2008 Aliyah Schick

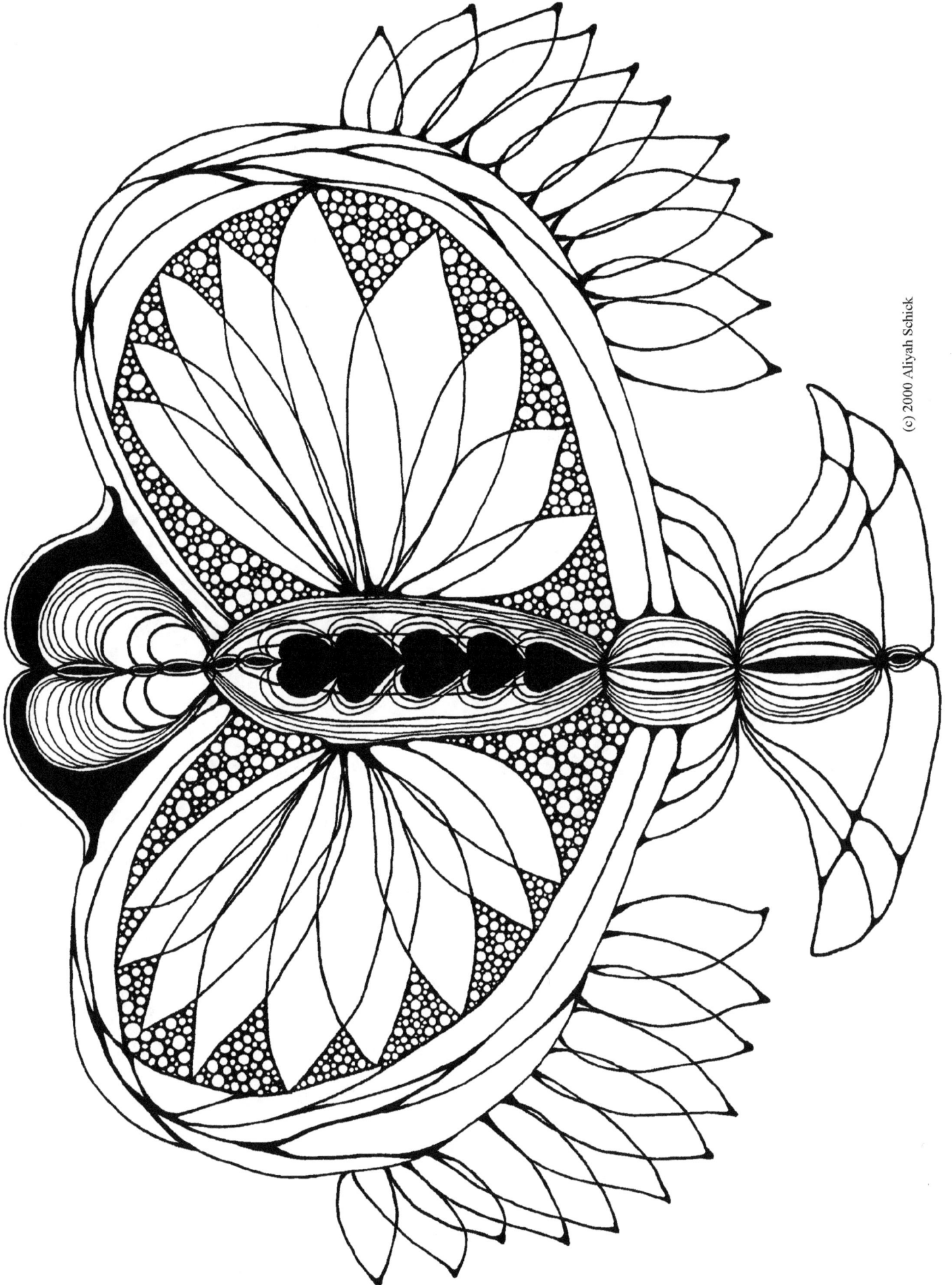

49

Meditative Impressions

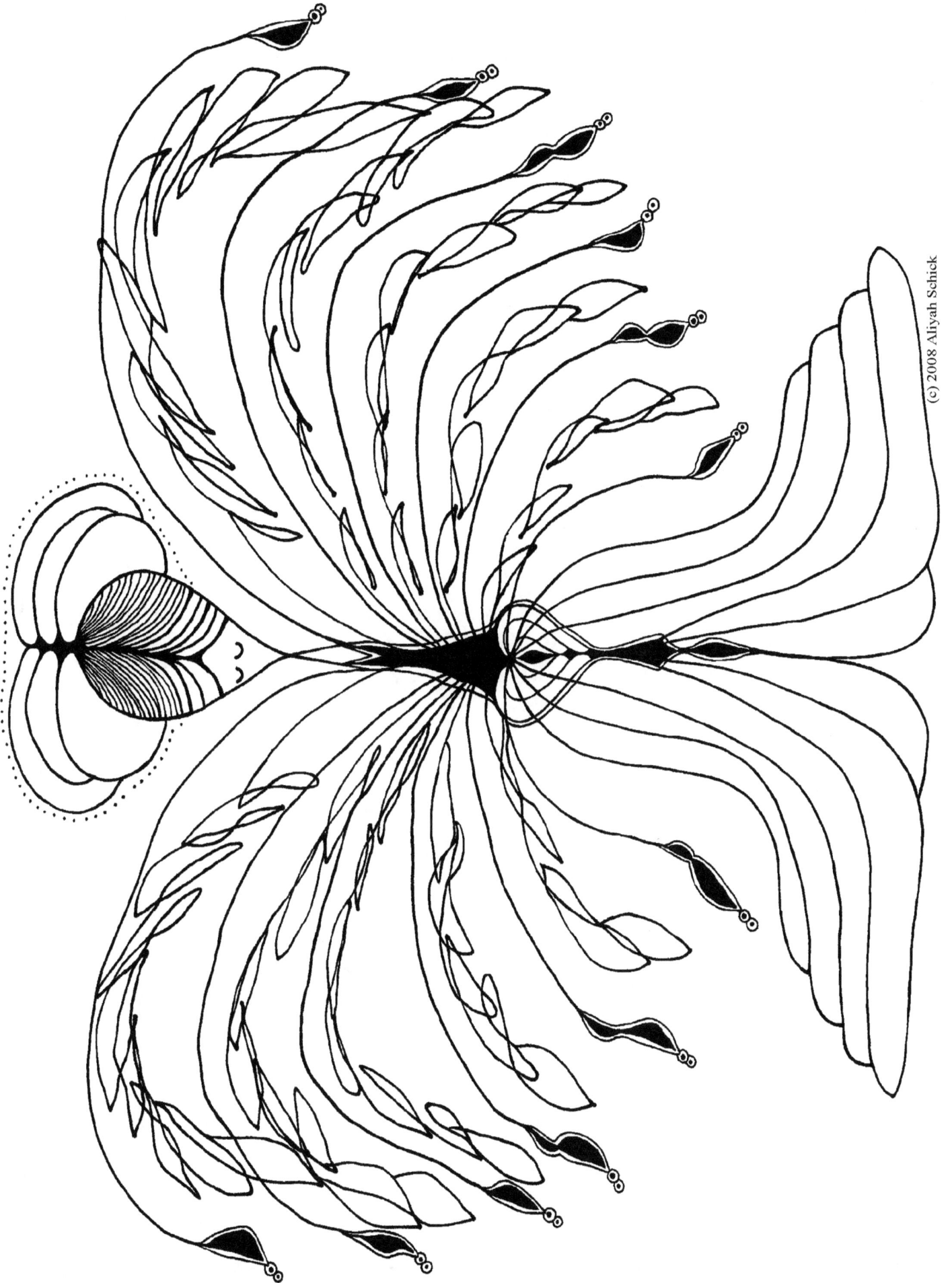

51

53

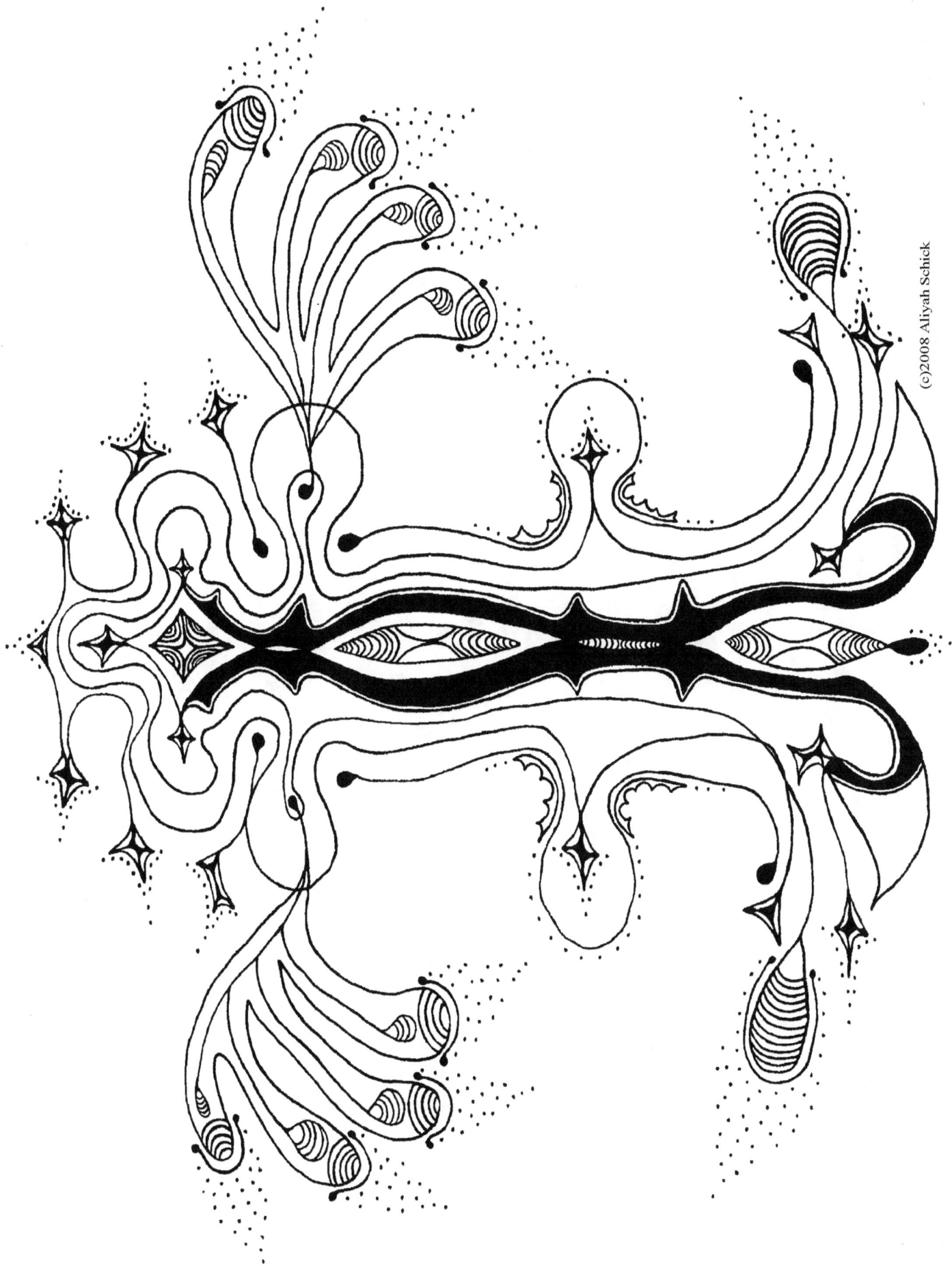

Meditative Impressions

57

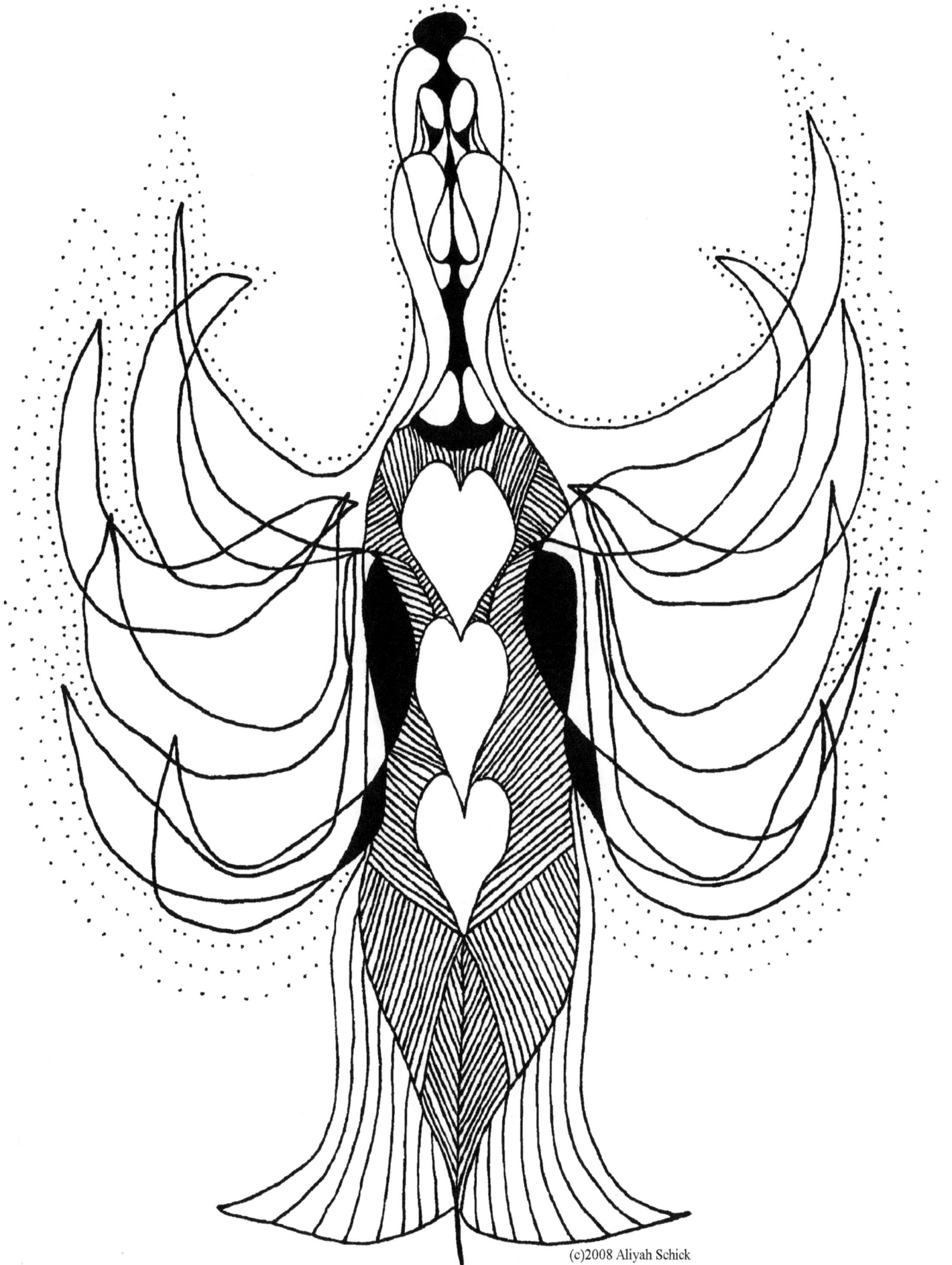

(c)2008 Aliyah Schick

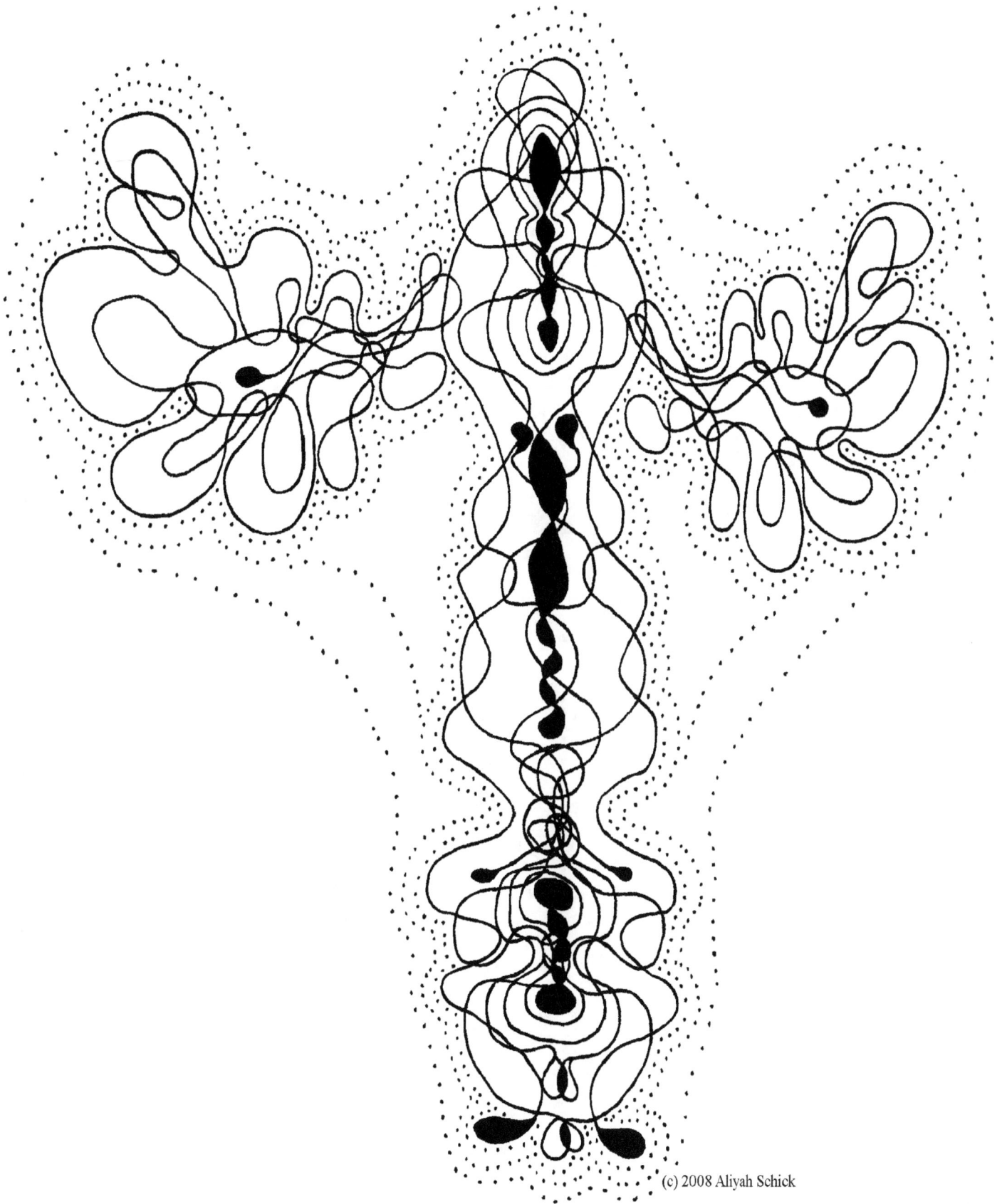

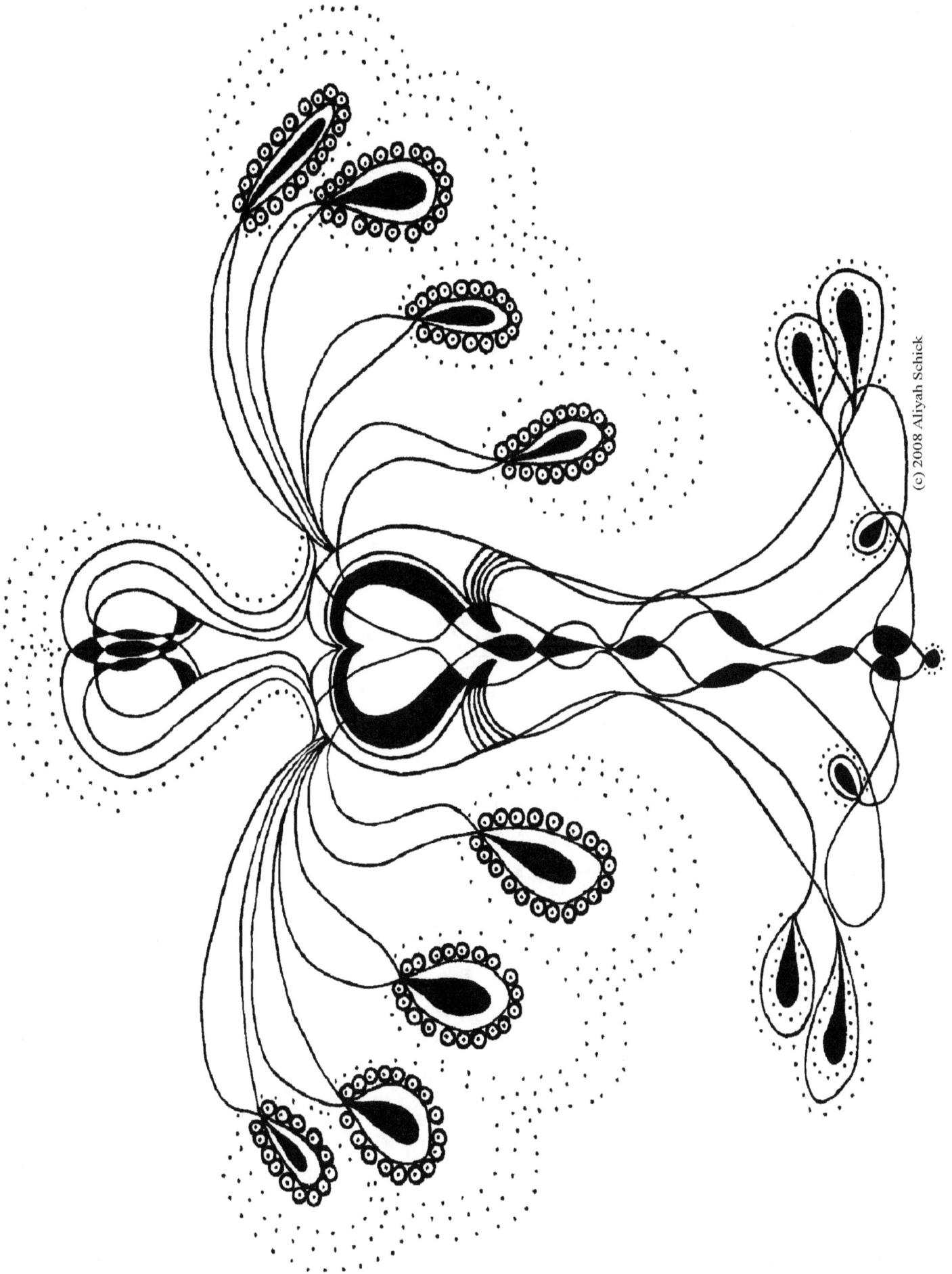

(c) 2008 Aliyah Schick

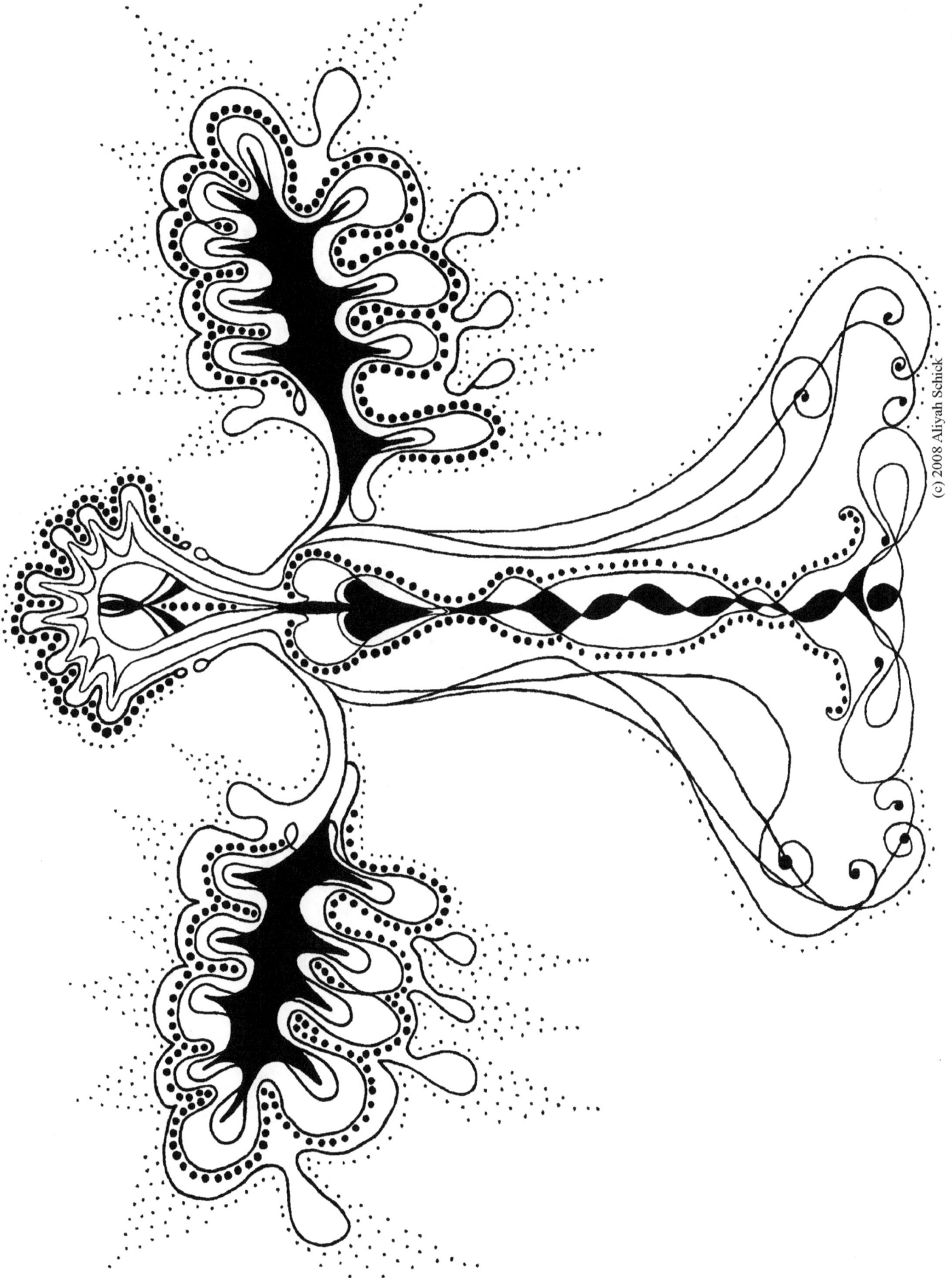

Meditative Impressions

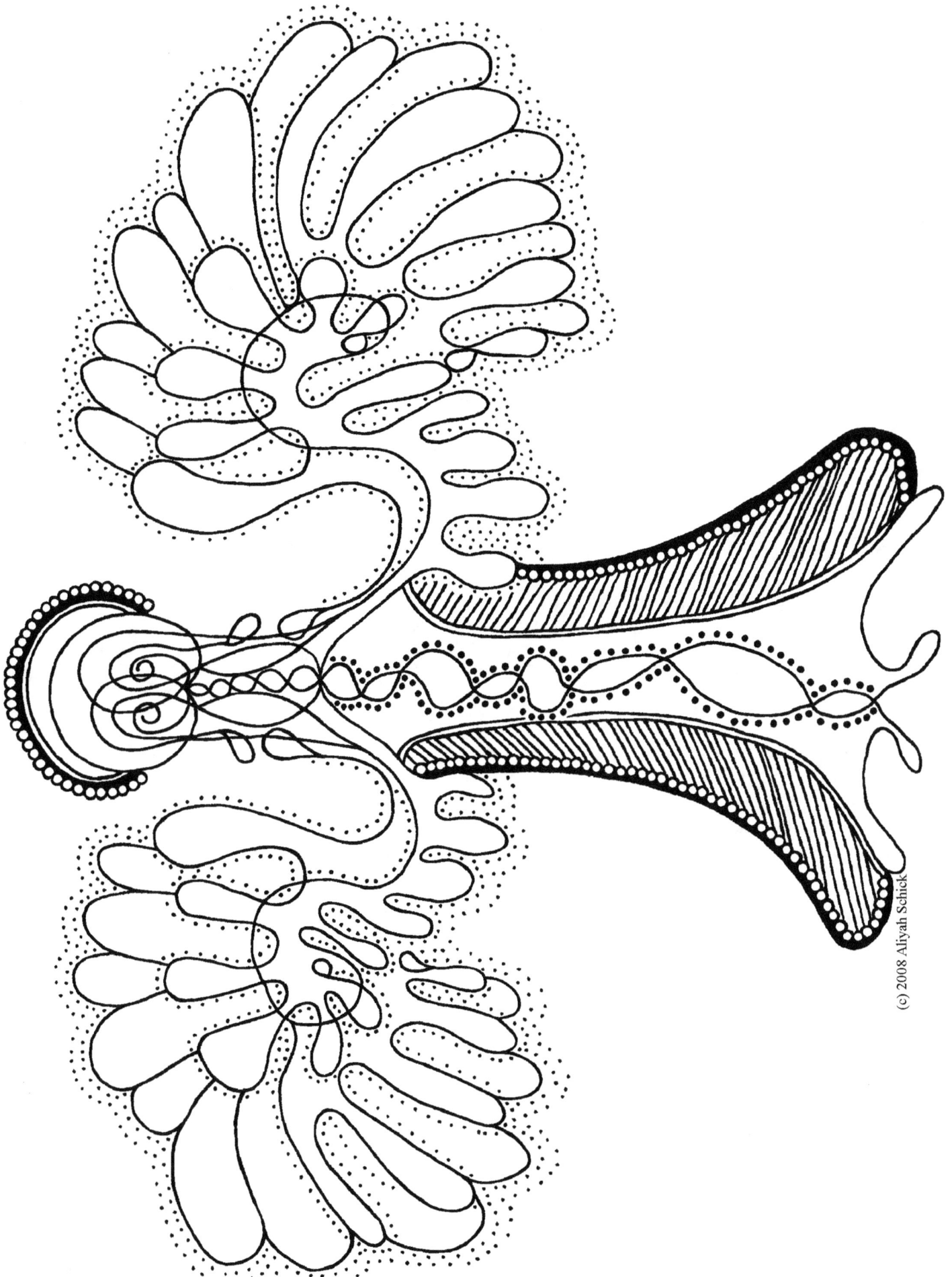

69

(c) 2008 Aliyah Schick

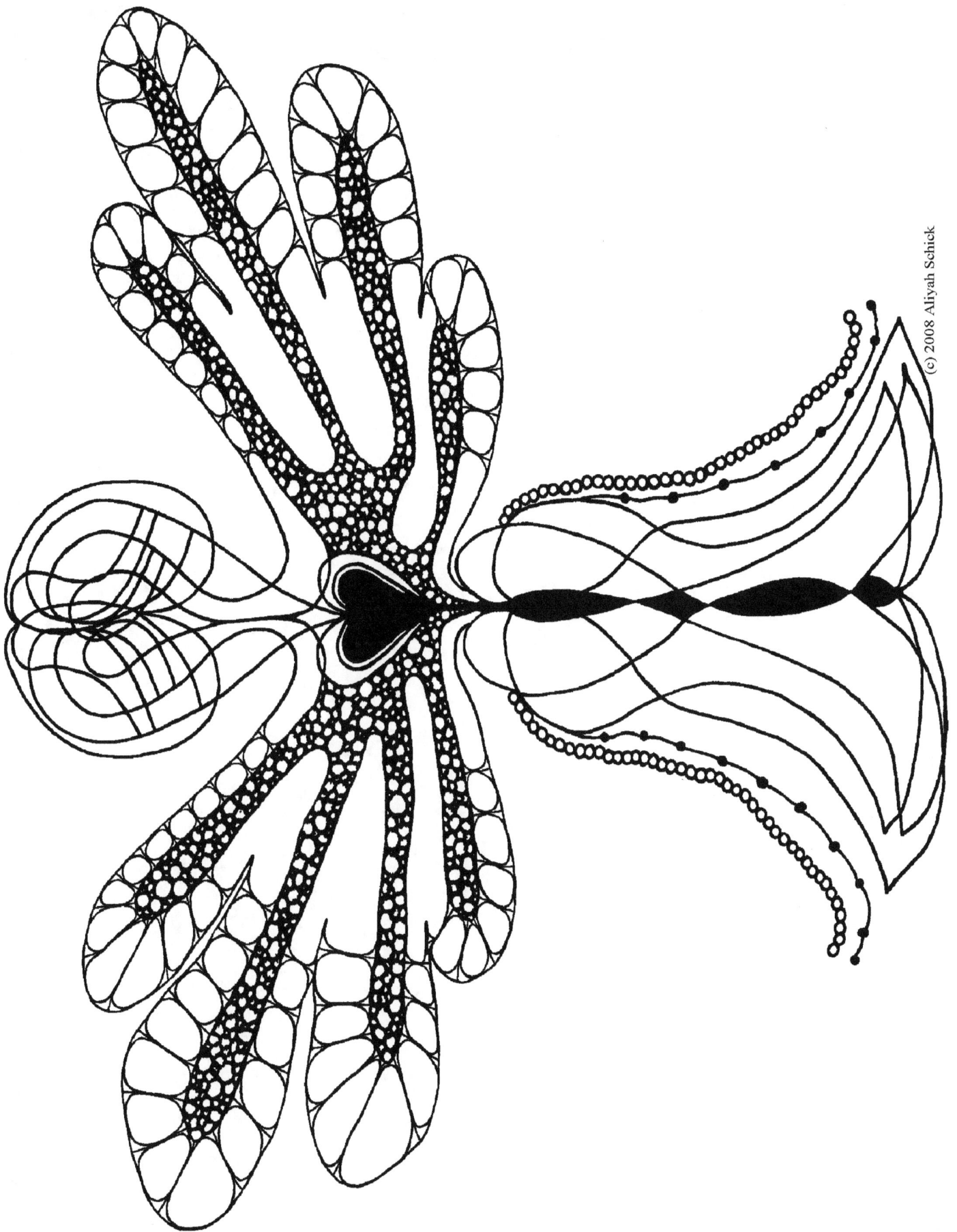

71

Meditative Impressions

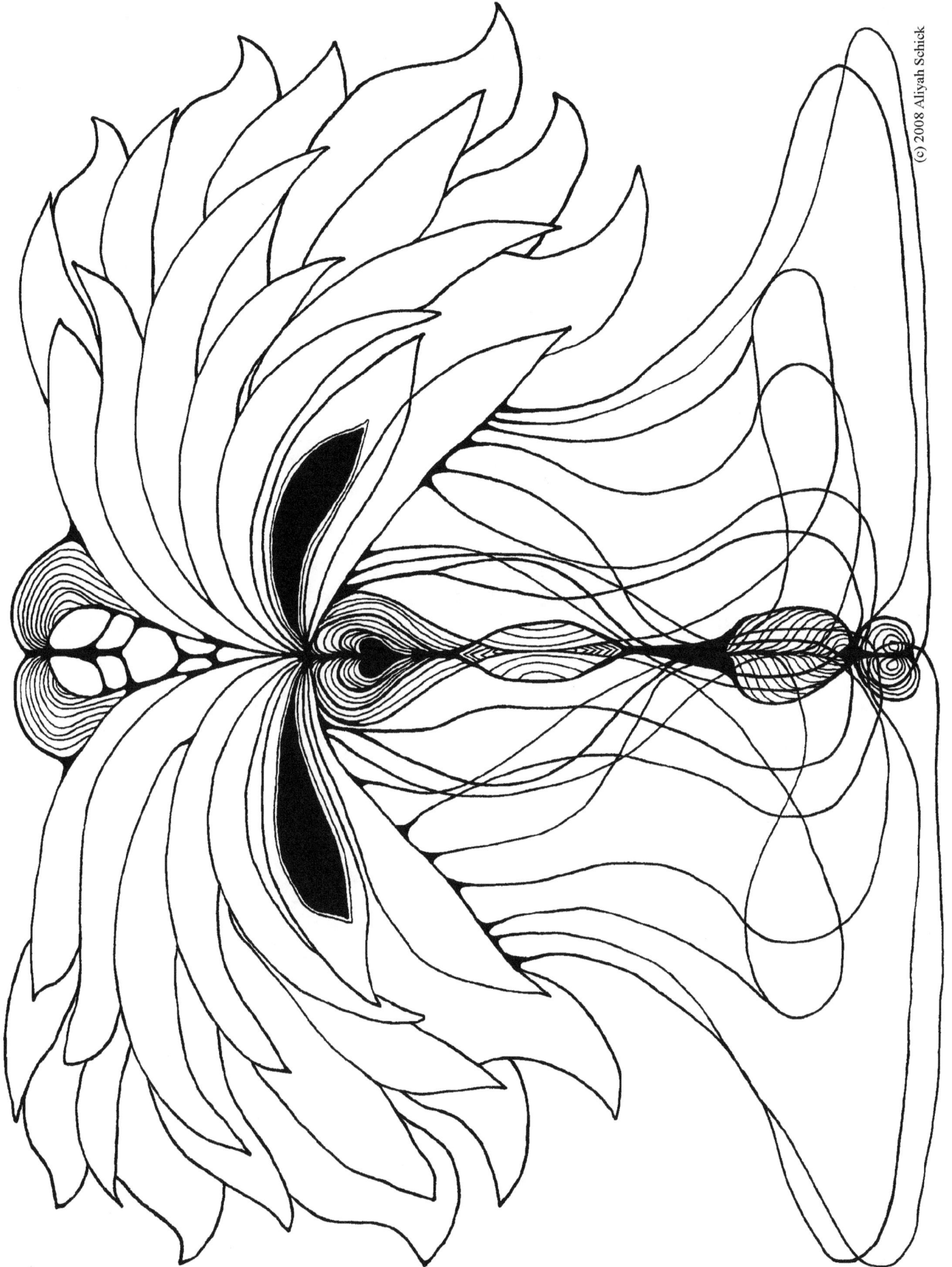

Meditative Impressions

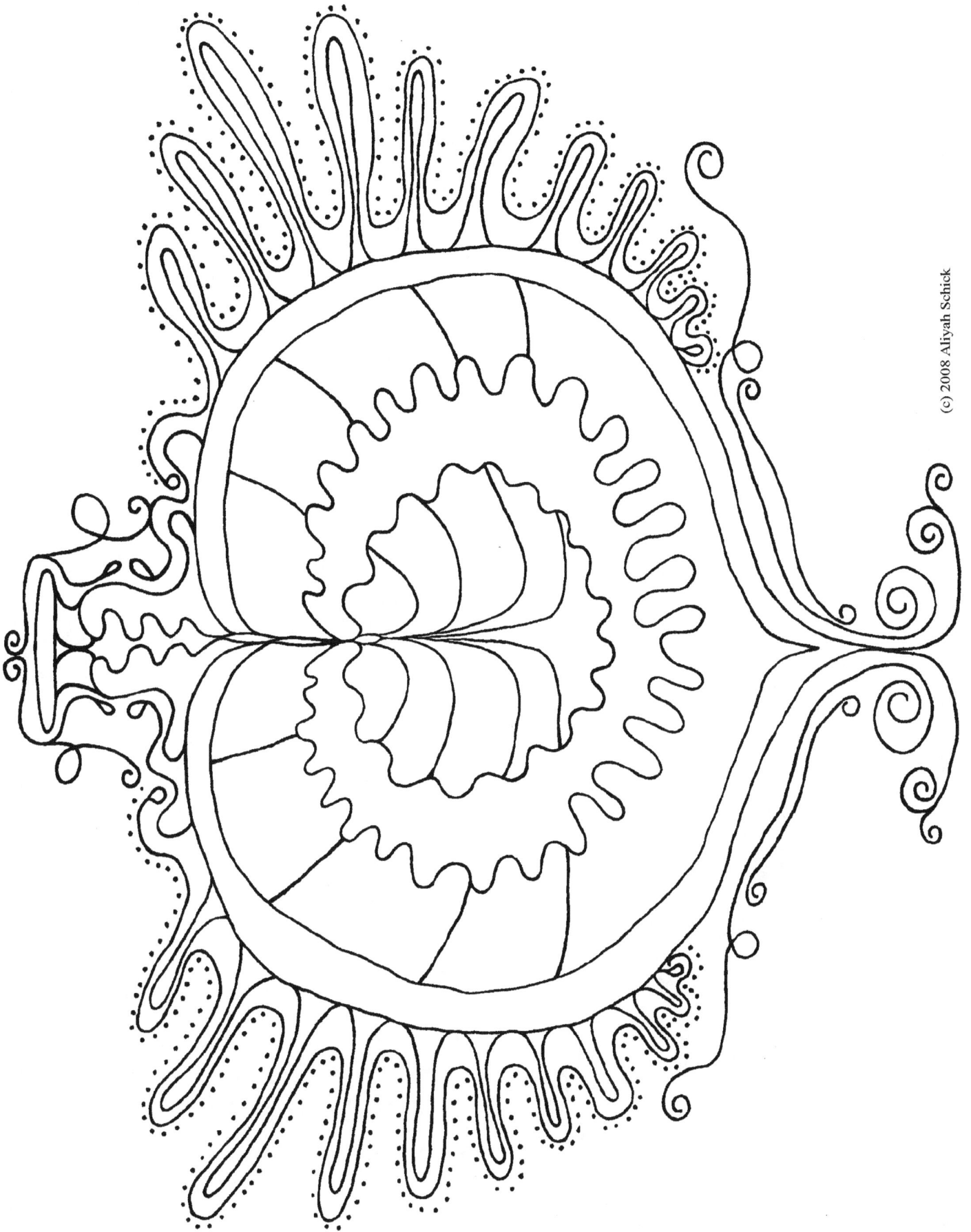

The Sacred Imprints™ Meditative Coloring Books
Five Volumes: Angels, Crosses, Ancient Symbols, Hearts, and Labyrinths

---

Meditative Coloring Book 1 -- Angels

The Sacred Imprints ™ Angelic images are drawn during a centering meditation. With a pen in each hand, Aliyah allows the lines to go where they will, the two sides mirroring each other. Every movement is guided by spirit; every drawing is different; and each one is a wonderful surprise filled with angelic presence.

Meditative Coloring Book 2 -- Crosses

The cross is one of our most ancient and enduring sacred symbols, found in nearly every culture throughout human existence. It symbolizes the celestial, spirtual divine coming into being in this material world. It represents God taking form, and the integration of soul into physical life. The drawings of the Crosses Series feature ancient and contemporary images of the cross in reflections of the deep spiritual significance of its form.

Meditative Coloring Book 3 -- Ancient Symbols

Ancient and indigenous sacred images speak deeply to us, to our bellies and our bones, to our cellular memory and our wisdom, to our souls' yearnings. Native peoples throughout time and place see the sacred in all of life. For them, holiness is life and life is holiness. Life is the manifestation of the holy in all things. The drawings of the Ancient Symbols Series feature timeless designs used by every culture on earth to remind us of the sacred.

Meditative Coloring Book 4 -- Hearts

The heart is one of our favorite symbols, evoking feelings of love, caring, loyalty, and devotion. As you spend time with these Sacred Imprints Heart drawings, open your heart to live with more compassion for others and for yourself. Open your life to deeper connection with the earth and all of life. Open yourself to recognize the sacred in all things, including in yourself.

Meditative Coloring Book 5 -- Labyrinths

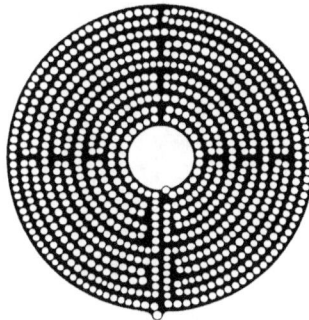

These original artist's labyrinth drawings invite you to color your steps into the labyrinth, one by one, as you contemplate, meditate, or pray. Go deep into your inner wisdom and guidance where questions' answers reveal themselves and choices come clear. Or simply relax and be with your breathing. Now you can bring your labyrinth with you to wherever you need to be.

www.MeditativeColoring.com

www.ingramcontent.com/pod-product-compliance
Lightning Source LLC
LaVergne TN
LVHW081320060426
835509LV00015B/1600